Aaron B. Thompson

Morning Songs

Aaron B. Thompson

Morning Songs

ISBN/EAN: 9783337265571

Printed in Europe, USA, Canada, Australia, Japan

Cover: Foto ©Thomas Meinert / pixelio.de

More available books at **www.hansebooks.com**

MORNING SONGS.

BY

Aaron Belford Thompson.

PRINTED AND FOR SALE BY THE AUTHOR.

ROSSMOYNE, OHIO.

1899.

INTRODUCTION.

Having written a number of poems in my leisure,
I have been prevailed upon by friends to pub
-lish them; yielding to their solicitations I here by
extend this little volume entitled, Morning Songs'
to the public, and hope it will prove satisfactory
to my readers.

THE AUTHOR.

~~~~~~~~~~~~~~~~~~~~~~

AARON BELFORD THOMPSON.

TO

My dear Sisters,

CLARA and PRISCILLA,

In memory of true and tender affection,

And in testimony of

Increasing love and gratitude,

This Volume is Dedicated

BY

THE AUTHOR.

INVOCATION

Oh gracious Master, just and true,
    With all Thy wondrous plans,
Lead us, a trodden nation, through
    This dark and stormy land!

Thou who didst hear our father's cry,
    Midst suffering pain and woe,
Who dried the tear drops from their eye,
    Can guide us as we go.

Let not our hearts with trouble wake,
    And say there is no way,
The hour before the morning break,
    Gives little hope of day.

Oh let this be the darkest hour,
    Which vails the dawning light;
And let us trust Jehovah's power,
    Till daybreak fades the night.

(5)

NEW JERUSALEM.

Behold that New Jerusalem!
  Her streets are paved with gold;
Twelve stately gates, are set with pearls,
  And yet the half's not told.

Great walls of rich and precious stones,
  Surround that city fair;
Sweet music from that heavenly clime,
  Swells out upon the air.

Within those walls so beautiful,
  The heaven immortals dwell;
What peace and comfort they enjoy,
  No mortal tongue can tell.

The sun within those walls that shine,
  Is He who's glorifed;
Splendor and glory's all combine,
  In Him for nations died.

And all those gates of pearl and gold,
  Forever stand ajar;
To welcome strangers passing by,
  Where nothing can debar.

There shall my weary soul find rest,
  Where blissful joys abound;
Around His throne so pure and blest,
  I'll lay my trophies down.

OUR GIRLS.

A song to the damsels, our Ethiope maids!
   Her crisp curly locks, in beauty arrayed.
Her voice is so gentle, so tender so true;
   Her smiles glow like sun-beams;
     Her eyes spark like dew.

Her teeth shine like pearls, her laughter the while,
   Re-echoes with music, like waves on the Nile;
Her steps are so gentle, kindhearted is she;
   The Ethiope maid, is the damsel for me.

No paints and no powder, bedecks her sweet face;
   Her beauty is nature, the rarest of grace.
The oils and pomatums, ne'er touches her hair;
   Those curled raven locks, by nature are there.

Before ev'ry nation, exultant we'll sing;
   Arrayed in her beauty, our maids we will bring.

(8)

A BIRTHDAY TRIBUTE.

Walking through life's tranquil journey,
    Flowers blooming 'neath her feet;
She have reached each year a milestone,
    Stationed on life's highway street.

On and on, old time hath led her,
    Through the night, and through the day,
In her childhood's joys, and sorrows,
    As the milestones pass away.

On each one her name is written,
    And life's journey briefly told;
Of her infancy and childhood,
    Written in the purest gold.

And her cup with many a blessing,
    Have been filled from year to year.
She 've been blessed, with friends and
kindreds;
    And a loving father's care.

(9)

And a sympathetic mother,
  Who have loved so dear since birth;
Sharing all her pains and sorrows,
  Sharing all her joys and mirth;

She have reached the twentieth milestone,
  'Long her blooming path of life,
She hath grown a handsome lady,
Soon she'll face a nobler strife.

And we've met to pay her homage,
  Friends and kindreds, all around;
'Tis our debt that we should wish her,
  All the joys that can be found.

May life's journey in the future,
  Be more radiant than the past;
And the purest light from heaven,
In her pathway e'er be cast.

(10)

BEYOND THE RIVER.

Just beyond the brimming river,
   Just beyond the flowing tide,
I have thoughts within me ever,
   Of rare scenes on yonder side.

Days and months and years are fleeting;
   Still that stream is passing on;
Pilgrims, saints, and angels greeting,
Those who just have past beyond.

We are journeying to that river;
   Some have reached the flowing tide;
Some have crossed to 'turn no never;
   From the scenes on yonder side.

Some have scarce begun their journey;
   Some have trudged it faint and slow;
Some have reached the topmost mountain,
Looking on the vale below,

They can see the brimming river;
　How divide her banks between,
Where the parting friends doth sever,
　Ford the tide to realms unseen.

I have dearest friends who've left me,
　And have crossed that whelming flood;
Left their all, their earthly duty,
　And have gone to meet their God,

Where 'tis said, the sun shines ever;
　And the trees forever green;
Where there's grief and parting never,
　Oh! that Beulah land unseen.

When I've trod life's dreary highway,
　Footsore, weary, lame and slow,
When I've climbed the mountain's summit,
　When I've reached the vale below,

May I cross that brimming river,
　Fearless of its mighty flood;
Leave my earthly cares forever,
　Cross with joy to meet my God.

OUR NATIONAL FLAG.

Noble flag, in triumph flowing,
   O'er this land where now we be,
With thy glorious colors showing,
   Flag of truth, I'll sing of thee.

Many a year you've shone your splendor,
   Stationed on the highest towers;
Where the sounds of music tender,
   Mounts the breeze through leafy bowers.

Thou hast shone thy might and duty,
   In the present and the past;
   Thou hast faced the storm with beauty,
Faced the tempest's furious blast.

Oft before the deadly cannon,
   Fell brave soldiers mangled, slain,
Floating steadfast in thy mammon,
   Floated at old Lundy's lane.

(13)

While amidst the rush, the hurry,
    Midst the musketry sublime,
Lark shrill notes the fife rang merry;
    With a zeal you've beat the time.

Many a noble gallant warrior,
    Robed in red, the white, the blue,
In their tomb, awaits the morrow;
    'Neath the cold and chilling dew.

Now when blissful peace and pleasure,
    On our land and on our seas,
Still with stars and stripes keep measure,
    Floating on the balmy breeze.

Dearest flag, a debt, a duty,
    All this nation owes to thee;
As you flow with pride and beauty,
    With thy colors fair to see.

With our arms, we will protect thee;
    And our tongues shall speak thee true;
Flag of truth, most noble emblem;
    Decked with red, the white, the blue.

MY COUNTRY HOME.

Near the highway in a valley,
　Where sweet rose and poppies bloom,
Where cool shade and breezes rally,
　Stands my happy country home.

On her walls antique and rustic,
　Clings the vernal leafy vines;
In the yard so calm majestic,
　Grows the lovely columbines.

Orchard trees in vernal splendor,
　Shades the grassy carpet green,
And the song birds sing so tender;
　Hidden by the leafy screen.

Calm and peaceful stands the dwelling,
　While great beauty round I see,
And my thoughts with rapture swelling,
　Dawns a trodden path to me.

(15)

Dawns a path of thorns and roses;
   Dawns a path of joy and gloom;
Dawns the hour, o'er friends most dearest,
   Wept I at their burial tomb.

I reflect upon my childhood,
   Round this cottage I did play;
When far in the beechen wild-wood,
   Gathered I sweet flowers of May.

And I plucked the precious jewels,
   While this wood-land I did roam,
Wove them into radiant garlands;
   Brought them to my country home.

Long may stand this little cottage,
   She hath harbored me since birth;
Though the hue fades in her dotage,
   'Tis my dirtues home on earth.

EMANCIPATION.

Three cheers! well may we shout with joy,
   And hail Emancipaton;
Our fetters long have been destroyed :
   We are a free, free, nation.

No more like cattle on the hills,
   That feed upon the clover;
Shall wait our brethern for their doom,
   Unable to discover.

No more upon our brother's track.
   We'll hear the blood-hounds baying;
The cries of men to bring him back,
   With curse and evil sayings.

No more our maidens bought and sold,
   The southorn tyrant's booty;
No more the brutal trader's gold,
   Shall buy the sable beauty.

MORNING SONGS.

No more our brave and gallant youths,
   Shall tremble of the morrow;
Behold, sweet liberty and truth,
   Hath broke the chains of sorrow.

For now we stand on freedom's plain,
   With joy and exultation:
Though scarred and maimed,
   From bondage chain,
   We'll hail Emancipation.

Three cheers! we'll shout our liberty:
   Long may our nation live,
Large, large, may grow her fruitful tree,
   And sweetest manna give.

THE DREARY DAY.

The clouds creep low, the day is dark;
  The wind howls sad and drear;
The rain desends with glittering spark;
  No cheerful sunlight near.

The orchard trees, their leaves all drenched,
  Bends low their vernal crown;
The furtile soil her thirst have quenched,
  But still the rain comes down.

Oh dreary day! filled to the brim,
  The brooklet struggles on;
The mist, the fog, so dark, so dim;
  Oh! where is sunlight gone?

That glittering orb, once lit the land,
  With splendor, bright and clear;
Through stormy clouds his light grows wan;
  Have nature lost her cheer?

(19)

MORNING SONGS.

Deep in my melancholy breast,
  There comes a tranquil voice;
A gentle murmur pure and blest,
Which bids my soul rejoice.

The fair muse caught the cheering phrase,
  Which sounds like vesper chimes;
Her pen retraced a fiery blaze,
  In feet of rhythmic rhymes.

I read, and in my weary soul,
  The sun shone in again;
No more life's gloom about me roll,
  Though fall the dreary rain.

MY QUEEN.

Queen of my heart, of thee I am thinking;
Thinking, of thee through life's dreary
   dream;
Bright in my thoughts as the stars that
   are twinkling,
Shines thy fair image so calm and serene.

All day I have roamed through wood-land
   and meadow,
Seeking the beauty of nature's sweet flowers;
In the calm noon tide, reposed in the shadow
But ne'er found such beauty, among the
   green bowers.

Queen of my heart, for thee I am longing;
Longing to view thy beauty and grace;
Rare is thy beauty, to thee e'er belonging;
Sweet are the smiles on thy dear, winsome,
   face.

Love is divine;with love I adore thee;

  Fair,sable damsel,to thee I'll be true;

As thy companion,for e'er I'd be happy;

Thou gem of my casket that sparkles like

                    dew.

MORNING SONGS.

THE CHIMING BELLS.

Ho!watchman,from you belfry tower,
   Ring out those bells to me!
And let my fancies catch the power,
   That steals upon my soul each hour,
While chimes their melody.

I love to hear those chiming bells:
   To me,their music clear,
Time after time,strange stories tell,
   And oft they ring the parting knell,
Of friends and kinsmen dear.

And oft when at the alter stood,
   The modest bride,the groom,
Sweet echoes filled the vernal wood;
   Where giant oak and elm trees stood,
While zephers shook their plumes.

I love their sweet melodious chime,
   It wakes my sleeping soul;
They bear good news from heavenly clime.
   It cheers the heart,uplifts the mind,
When e'er those bells doth toll.

23

I love to hear their medley sound,
Swell on the sabbath morn:
Their music from yon tower, sinks down,
Into my heart with joy profound,
And banish cares forlorn.

Oft:imes in peace and quiet bliss,
The raptured music falls,
My soul craves for the parting kiss,
And yearns to break that vale of mist,
Which binds her like a thrall.

They swell with music sweet and clear,
Upon each mortal's breast;
Our doom advances near and near,
Those bells shall ring year after year,
When we are laid to rest.

Ho! watchman, ring those bells to me!
And let their music fall,
With chime and glee, o'er land, o'er sea,
In blissful peace to all.

THE CHAIN OF BONDAGE.

Arise! arise! my fellow-men,
Arise, with might and main;
  Arise, with intellectual din,
And cast aside your chains!

For, like a web around us bound,
This chain hath long entwined;
  It brought a mighty nation down,
And humbled low their minds.

How oft we're quelled when tempt to rise,
    By envy and disdain;
And ofttimes wipe our tearful eyes,
And try no more our chains.

Oh! tear them loose in union's strength!
We'll not be trampled down;
  We'll reach the promise land at length,
Behold the Ethiope's crown!

LEAD ME.

Lead me, oh my blessed Redeemer!
  Ere my feet shall walk astray;
Through this world of dire temptation,
  Lead me on the heavenly way!

Lead me, though my steps should faulter,
  As I journey through this land;
When I meet with worldly conflicts,
  Grasp me tighter by the hand.

On the verge of earth's temptation,
  When my strength is almost gone,
Haste before I fall, dear Savior,
  Grasp my hand and lead me on!

In my earthly joys and sorrow,
  Let me not forget the way!
For too soon may dawn the morrow,
  Should my steps be lead astray.

THE BUTTERFLY.

The butterfly with gorgeous hue,
  Flits noiseless through the summer air;
He sips the honey from the dew,
  And from the wild flowers fair.

Thus day by day, he soars abroad,
  O'er wood-land, hill and dale;
And e'er his restless flight affords,
  Sweet blossoms to regale.

From east to west, from north to south,
  He takes his aerial flight;
Ne'er 'till the summer sun is set,
  He shelters for the night.

And at the rising of the sun,
  When birds begin to sing,
He sallies from his hiding place,
  To dry his moisted wings.

He soars abroad, his wings now dry,
   His beauty still remains;
Now slow, and now with speed he flies;
   His days are all the same.

I'd envy him of hue and flight,
   But seeing his abode,
I learned that life in public sight,
   Is not what private showed.

And when declining days did come,
   He lost his tint of hue;
And trembling in his humble home,
   Did perish in the dew.

THE ONE I KNOW.

There's a gentle vioce like music;
  From a being kind and true;
There's a smile like glowing sunbeams,
  Sparkling on the summer dew.

There's a footstep calm and gentle;
  Lighter than a faries'tread;
Two bright eyes,of jet black beauty;
  Ebon locks bebecks her head,

Tiny hands so small but useful;
  Busy all the livelong day;
Toiling in her joys and sorrows,
  Toiling on a pilgrim way.

Ebon face bedecked with beauty;
  Form most graceful to behold;
Not one tith would be her value,
  Should I give my weight in gold.

THE SAME OLD SUN.

The same old sun is shining,
  That shone in Bethlehem;
That dawned upon the morning,
  When Christ our Saviour came.

His splendor is no brighter,
  His rays are spread the same,
As spread with gold on the streets of old,
  Where He healed the deaf and lame.

The same old sun is shining,
  That shone on Galilee;
When He called two angling brothers,
  And said, "Lo, follow me."

While down that dusty highway,
  The same old blazing sun;
Shone down upon my Saviour's brow,
  And on Capernaum.

(30)

And at the Jordan river,
  This sun shone bright and free,
When He to John, who stood amazed,
  Said, "Suffer it to be."

Through the land of old Judea,
  Through neighboring cities round,
Where e'er there went our Saviour,
  The same old sun shone down.

The same old sun was shining,
  When He 'fore Pilate stood:
Where sat the false accusers,
  Who yearned to shed His blood.

As they hailed Him king with scoffing,
  Robed Him with purple gown,
The radiant light of the golden sun,
  In silence glittered down.

And on the road to Calvary,
  With thorn wreath on His brow,
The same old sun was shining down,
  That shines upon us now.

But when upon that fatal cross,
    When the pang of death passed through,
Vile earthquakes,shook this sinful earth,
    This sun was hid from view.

And round His tomb upon that morn,
    When weeping Mary came,
The sun renewed his brilliant light,
    That glittering orb of flame.

And when an angel rolled the stone,
    And to that mother said,
"He've rose, He's gone to Galilee;
    Come, see where He hath layed."

Behold, with glittering beams of gold,
    This sun gleamed round Him then,
"All power is mine,"He bravely told,
    "Go! preach my word to men."

Still shines the same old blazing sun,
    He runs his course each day;
While nations perish one by one,
    He shines upon their clay.

THE SUMMER NIGHT.

Balmy are the breezes blowing,
  Low the sun sinks in the west;
Cattle far and near are lowing,
  Homeward,seeks the plowman rest.

Flowers that shone in gorgeous beauty,
  'Neath the summer,shining sun,
Droop their heads repose with nature,
  Close their petals one by one.

While the lark and feathered songsters,
  Shelters in their leafy nest,
· Gaze upon the fading twilight,
  Gaze upon the golden west.

And when sleep the weary songsters,
When through dream-land,takes their flight,
  All the air is filled with beings,
Borne upon the wings of night.

Fire-flies with enchanted lanterns,
  Through the darkened gloom they come :
Close behind pursues the beetle,
  With a steadfast noisy hum.

And the screech-owl's cry re-echoes,
Through the moor-land, through the swamp;
  Through the forest and the fallow,
Boldly doth the wild-fox tramp.

Far among the stars an echo,
  Borne upon the zephyrs still,
Falls into my ear so faintly,
'Tis the notes of whip-poor-wills.

While the ponderous orbs in heaven,
  Twinkles with a silvery light,
And the air, all filled with calmness,
  Welcome, be ye summer night!

I AM GLAD.

I am glad that I drank at the Fountain;
  From its waters I found a relief:
And that stream from Calvary's mountain,
  Have healed my affliction and grief.

How I thirst when I roamed o'er the desert,
  And viewed the oasis before:
I journeyed through heat and through
                          sand-storm,
And oft for sweet waters deplored.

But at length I arrived at the Fountain,
  Though footsore and blind from the sand;
Blessed stream ot Calvary's mountain,
  O'er the banks of the channel it ran.

I drank of it's life healing waters,
  With a sparkle like pearl it did gleam,
My thirst was there quenched, and rejoicing,
  I bathed in that life's given stream.

THE OAK TREE.

By the river that is flowing,
   Towards the ocean's tide,
Stands an oak tree, tall, gigantic,
   Branches spreading wide.

And his form so tall and stately,
   Brace the cool spring breeze,
With his crown so bright and vernal,
   King of all the trees.

Grayhaired men, now old and palsied,
   Once in childhood played,
'Neath this oak tree by the river,
   Where the acorns layed.

Through the wear of many a summer,
   Wax childhood to man,
Same in valorous strength and beauty,
   Still the oak tree stands.

And his leaves hath yield to autumn,
   Many a century year,
When the red men roved the forest,
   Chased the panting deer.

MORNING SONGS.

Oft there floated down the river,
  In his snug canoe,
Indian youth with bow and quiver:
  Here, the wildbirds flew.

And the fox with tearless footsteps,
  Roamed the forest here,
Deer and fawn, beneath the moon-light,
  Grazed with little fear.

All alone the oak tree standeth,
  Now the forest's gone,
Ne'er the scenes of wood-land nature,
  Left to look upon.

Birds migrated, flowers created,
  Red men came and gone;
Time hath like the flowing river,
  Drift to parts unknown

Still he holds his youthful beauty,
  Wears his broad, green crown;
As a landmark he's now standing,
  Known for miles around.

THE FORESIGHT.

Behold, the time advances,
　It's nearing day by day;
And I view a gleam of sunlight,
　Through a mist and stormy way.

The hour is fast approaching,
　As the Book of Truth records,
When the hand of Ethiopia,
　Shall weal her trusty sword.

Not with stern and brutal sovereign,
　Not with blood-stained hands of might,
But in freedom's name she'll govern,
　With justice, truth, and right.

Though Caucasia's tongues deride us,
　In their 'tempt to make us fall,
But God who loves His children,
　Looks upon us, one and all.

And through His precious promise,
　Like a dark and misty vail,
Behold, a ship comes sailing,
　With rainbow-tinted sails.

The pilot at his rudder,
　　With cold and bleeding hands,
Long stood with fear and trembling,
　　While lost upon the strand.

And oft he lowers the anchor,
　　At night fall on the deep,
Or when the storms are raging,
　　His trusty vigils keep;

Through the darkest fog before him,
　　Which vails the light before,
He stands the howling tempest,
　　And looks for yonder shore.

Across the stormy waters,
　　Though the winds come down with might,
Ere long the pilot on that ship,
Shall see a gleaming light.

The dawn of day advances,
　　'T will calm the rolling sea,
Like the Hand that calmed the tempest,
　　On the lake of Galilee.

I view her in my vision,
  Her shipmates and her crew,
With trusty hopes are waiting,
  To anchor at yon view.

Though many a gallant shipmate,
  Who were drowned in the dreadful deep,
Lay buried 'neath the waters;
In their aqueous graves they sleep.

  I see one brave old sailor,
  Who has climbed the topmost mast,
And he shouts with loud, Hosanna,
  At the scenes before him cast.

She's heading for yon harbor,
  Her sails are now unfurled,
Though drenched, and shaken by the winds,
  Her splendor awes the world.

Their dawns another vision,
  And the Muses bid me write,
I see her in the harbor,
  Her sails are sparkling bright.

I see Queen Ethiopia,
   Before all nations stand,
She is robed in royal purple,
   And a seal is in her hand.

As she lifts her hand, with jewels,
   To take the solemn vow,
Kings, prince, and nobles, hail her,
   All nations 'fore her bow.

THE SHINING STAR.

Shine on, bright stars with sparkling light!
   Shine in yon heavenly dome,
Illume the skies, with splendor bright,
   In my celestial home!

Ye sparkling gems, of sapphire hue,
   That stud the skies afar,
All glowing like the summer's dew,
   Shine on, ye faithful stars!

Shine on, for as I view the sight,
   Thy bright gleam cast before,
My weary soul yearns for that Light,
   Which shines from heaven's bright shore.

It is a bright, and glorious star,
   Whose splendor o'er us fall,
My soul perceives it from afar,
   His light illumes them all.

It gives the color to the flowers,
   Whose odor sweet doth yield:
Provides with nourishment each hour,
   The lilies of the field.

(42)

And weary travelers 'neath this Light,
   Day after day are led;
Their blinded eyes receive new sight,
   Their hungry souls, are fed.

 Then spread abroad thy glorious light,
   With rarest blessings stored!
Illume my weary soul by night,
   With peace and sweet accord!

THE FEAST.

Come, the feast is spread and waiting,
    'Tis a message from the King;
Come, and thus partake ye needy,
    Come, and all your friends do bring!

'Tis a feast where all's invited,
    Rich and poor, the great, the small,
And the traveler lone, benighted,
    And the bearer of the pall.

Come, ye blind ones, lepers crawling,
    Come, ye halt, and come, ye lame!
For the message still is calling,
    Dine into the halls of fame!

Come and dine, for great the table,
    Many the vacant places still;
Throngs the rich, the poor, disabled,
    Yet the Master's hall's not filled.

THE SONG BIRD.

There's a music sweet and low,
　From a song-bird in the west;
And the sweet notes gently flow,
　From her little, leafy nest.
'Tis a song I've often heard,
　But I cannot catch the words,
While the cadence sweetly echoes pure
　　　　　　　an l blest.

When the sun sinks in the west,
　At the closing of the day,
And the golden beams aglow,
　I can hear her, far away;
I can hear her warble sweet,
　I can catch each note complete,
While I listen to that sweet and gentle lay.

Oft in melancholy mood,
　Blindly I the future brood,
　O'er some destination hidden from my view,
　Oft my heart is cheered like spring,
When her warble sweetly ring,
Through the haze of fading twilight and
　　　　　　the dew.

(45)

MORNING SONGS.

There's a sweeter music still,
From a song-bird 'mong the hills,
In a quiet country dwelling far away;
And her music thrilled with love,
Calm and gentle as a dove,
Lingering ever in my memory day by day.

'Tis a sable damsel fair,
Jet black curled, her raven hair,
And her beauty never changing stays the
same.
And her winsome, dusky face,
Marks her with divinest grace,
She's my sweet-heart;
But I will not tell her name.

SCENES OF LIFE.

As fade the evening twilight,
   Far in yon gleaming west,
And the plowman, and the reaper,
   Homeward-bound, to seek their rest,

Fades my childhood days, and fancies,
   Fades the vision of a child,
Fades the fairy tales and fictions,
   Once my childish thought beguiled.

Midst rare scenes of vanished fancies,
   Still remains in memory bright,
There are visions which enhances,
   Still to me a childish light.

Oft they shine o'er man's dominion,
   One brief instant then are flown,
Like the condor on his pinions,
   Mounts to summits scarcely known.

Soon the youthful might and valor,
   Of this form shall lose its sway,
Soon these eyes shall faintly glimmer,
   And this head be bent and gray.

(47)

MORNING SONGS.

Still among time's vast procession,
  March the multitude so brave,
Page, and sage of mark profession,
  Seeking but the solemn grave.

Day by day in this procession,
  I am pressing towards the van,
  While the fading days of childhood,
Change my youthful form to man.

So I'm pressed from man's dominion,
  Through the scenes of joy and gloom,
Till I mount death's direful pinions,
  Aged infirmed, a silent tomb.

FAREWELL TO SUMMER.

Farewell to the summer,
   Behold, she hath fled;
Her bright vernal foliage,
   Are faded and dead;
The hot, golden, sunbeams,
   Shine brisk through the trees;
The leaves on their pinions,
   Ascends on the breeze.

Farewell to the summer,
   For autumn is here,
The skies they are cloudy,
   The days dark and drear;
Wild winds like a deluge,
   Through fields shall desend,
The trees of their beauty,
   Must yield to the wind.

Farewell to the summer,
   The birds that are known,
For music and beauty,
Behold they have flown;

(49)

MORNING SONGS.

The caw of the crow, and the cry of the jay,
  Resounds through the wood-land,
    And fields far away.

Farewell to the summer,
  Sad, sad, my refrain,
Her beauty and splendor,
  Shall fade 'neath the rain;
All cloudy and dreary our days soon shall be,
  And the east winds shall howl,
  O'er meadow and lea.

Farewell to the summer, 'tis sad to depart,
  All thy charms they have vanished,
    Thy beauty and art;
The vines have grown crimson,
  On walls over head,
  Sweet odorous blossoms, are faded, and dead.

Farewell to the summer, long 'fore thy return
  Sad hearts, shall await thee,
For thee, they shall yearn;
  They shall honor thy beauty,
Of days long ago, and welcome thy coming,
Through the frost and the snow.

THE TRAVELER'S DREAM.

In the calm of the noontide, and silent the day,
    A traveler sat down for to rest;
  He bore in his hand a plat of the way,
    A rout seemed easy and best.

Full of zeal and of valor, this traveler had come,
    Through lands that were rugged and steep;
Midst music of birds, and the wildbee's hum,
Midst fragrance, that rose from the radiant
                    blooms,
    Through brooklets that flowed to the deep.

While footsore and weary, as he rest'neath the
                    shade.
    His eyelids soon shut in repose;
  In his vision and dream he saw a fair maid,
    Midst wreathes of blossoms and rose.

The eyes of the sleeper beheld in that dream;
    With marvel he looked on the sight,
Her raiments, their sheen were purple an green,
    And her jewels like stars of the night.

(51)

She drew near the stranger,
    She stretched forth her hand,
And thus did the traveler behold,
A plat with its highways, that led to a land,
That land was a city of gold.

But its route was so rugged, the hills were so
                                        steep,
And the highways were dreary, forlorn;
    There were tombs of travelers,
    In death they did sleep,
There were vines and brambles and thorns.

Fair damsel, he said to the beautiful maid,
Though my travels've been rugged and steep,
    Yet my path have been laid, with flowers
                            and with shade,
    Their odor and fragrance most sweet.

The end of my journey though my eyes
                            can't behold,
Yet I fain could observe from afar,
Should I look in yon future, a city of gold
With splendor as bright as a star.

Arise, said the damsel, and journey with me;

And soon on your path way we'll find,

That the fruits of thy toil through sunshine
and shade,

Leads not to a fate so sublime.

He seized her fair hand so they sped through
the land:

Cross plain, through valley and glen,

And soon in his dream, by a chasm did stand,

Beheld there his fate and the end.

He viewed from the brink as he paused
with the maid,

Horrid sights, as he gasped for his breath,

In that grim dreary depth through darkness
and shade,

He beheld an angel of death.

His wings were outspread and he soared
o'er the dead,

Where travelers, benighted had fell,

And the bones on the waste,

Of that vail thick were spread,

And the grim sights were startling to tell.

The traveler was frightened;

He groped for her hand to retrace o'er
the route she had lead,

All trembling and weary alone did he stand

He awoke, but the damsel had fled.

CALLING.

I have heard dear friends, a Saviour,
  Calling, calling, day by day;
Night and morning, noon and evening,
  Never ceasing, calls away.

When with mirth among my comrades,
  I do frolic and rejoice,
When I pause awhile at leisure,
  I can hear my Saviour's voice.

I can hear my Saviour calling,
  In the tranquil hours of night;
When the morn and silent noontide,
  Wakes the sun with golden light.

Heard His voice through earthly struggles,
  As I've shed a parting tear,
O'er dear friends, who've gone before me,
  As each moment fleets the year.

Though the din of earthly tumult,
  Loud into my ears doth fall,
Still I hear my Saviour's pleading,
  Hark! I hear His loving call.

- - -.

(54)

Shall I turn away unheeding,
  Slight His promise so secure,
While I hear my Saviour pleading,
  Pointing 'cross to Jordan's shore?

FLEETING TIME.

Time is fleeting, time is fleeting,
  Swiftly doth each moment fly
Scarcely-dawns the morn till even;
  Short we live till we must die.

Time is fleeting, time is fleeting,
  As the waters seek the sea,
So down life's stream we are drifted,
  Till we reach eternity.

Time is fleeting, time is fleeting,
  Let not follies lure us on,
And we waste our time with trifles,
  Till the bloom of life is gone,

Then with feeble steps and palsied,
  Down life's stream with empty hands,
Leaves no honor, leaves no title,
  Print no footsteps in the sand.

Let us estimate its value,
  While we through life's journey go,
Let us gather in our harvest,
  Ere the winter comes with snow.

DEATH OF ABSALOM

Throughout the courts and palace halls,
  Resounds a mighty warrior's call;
The notes from out his trumpet horn,
  Reechoes on the early morn;
Enchanted by its warlike sound,
  His gallant charger paws the ground,
And champs his bit with rage.

  All, summoned by bold Joab's call,
  Ten thousand soldiers, large and tall,
And archers with their bows in hand,
  Did form in line at his command.

Out through the swinging palace gates,
March valorous men with spears and plates,
And war-steeds robed in trappings gay,
  Canters and prance; their piercing neigh,
Commingles with the warrior's lay,
  In one harmonious sound.

While through the swinging gates they go,
  Footmen, with battle-ax and bow,
War-chariots bearing gallant knights,
Went up against the Israelites.

King David stood beside the gate,
  His trouble was a ponderous weight,
And while he breathes a silent prayer,
  His eyes the sign of weeping wear;
To passing captains one by one,
  He says, "deal gently with my son."

So Joab and his men of might,
  Arrayed their armies for the fight;
With spear and battle-ax they stood,
  Among the oaks of Ephriam's wood.

The traitorous Israelites came down,
  Upon King David's host;
Amidst defying trumpet sound,
  Throughout the wood, and waste around,
Fell men by thousands, lost

The clashing of the sword and shield,
  Through Ephriam's wood resound;
Brave soldiers fell upon that field,
  And trampled by the horses' heel,
Lay prostrate on the ground.

War-steeds, blood-stained and riderless,
Down through the ranks, with fright did
press,
  Their eyes like fire, flashed left and right,
While captains urged their men to fight.

  And long before the set of sun,
A noble victory was won.

The blast of Joab's trumpet loud,
  Subdued the tumult of the crowd,
Brave warriors in their triumph came
  With broken sabers; men of fame,
With gory ax and broken shield,
  Returned victorious from that field.

  Out through the land the tidings
           spread.
  How Israel's traitorous host had fled;
How valorous men were overcome,
  The death of willful Absalom.

Upto the chamber o'er the gate,
  With breaking heart from troubles great,
He rose, and weeping as he went,
  In dire distress, his sad form bent,
His troubled soul most overcome,
  Cried, Absalom! Oh, Absalom!
Rebellious in thy youthful pride,
  Oh, that for thee, I could have died!

ON THE SOUTHERN SIDE.

On either side of the river's bank,
Sweet nature hath waken the bloom;
And the vernal trees, and the grasses rank,
Subdue drear winter's gloom.

As thunders along the turbulent tide,
To the end of her flow in the sea;
How little she know, that her channel
                              divides,
The land of the slave and the free.

The bondman ne'er ceased from his toil
                        in the corn,
He sang, yet the strains were not glee;
To the twilight of eve, from the dawn of
                        the morn,
He had gazed on the land of the free,

Long, long, had he toiled on the southern
                              shore,
And gazed on that flowing tide;
And ofttimes grim thraldom he sadly
                              deplored,
As he looked on the northern side.

(60)

But the rigorous law, and the river's flow,

Defied him to venture the tide,

For the hands of the spoiler, had threatened
the blow.
Should a bondman fail to abide.

No hopes for his freedom, his head decked
with gray,
Is bowed low with trouble and grief;

And his heart throbs with sighs,

As he longs for the day,

When death shall bring his relief.

BE READY.

Have your windows open, and your lamps
        trimmed and bright;
Put on the gospel armor of the purest white;

Keep the pickets at their duty,

In the highest towers and domes,

And be ye therefore ready; when the
        Bridegroom comes!

Have your windows open, and your lamps
        trimmed and bright;
For soon the day shall vanish;

And then dawns dreary night;

When the tempter prowls through darkness,

As a wild beast from its lair,

Where the watchman's light is gleaming,

He can never harm us there.

Have your windows open, and your la mps
        trimmed and bright;
Behold! the Bridegroom cometh,

 His raiments pure and white;

 He hath bid you to the table,

For the feast hath long been spread

So be ye therefore ready, to eat that living
        bread!

THE TEMPEST.

We have ofttimes heard in our childhood,
While perched on some old settler's knee,
Fanciful tales of the forest;
   And tales of the briny sea.

How the hunter that trudged through the
                  wood-land,
Returned when the sun's gleam was low,
Of drear battle-fields 'neath the moon light
Where fell the friend and the foe

The tales of the sea, they were many;
Of her sailors, her ebb and her flow,
Of the many ships lost in the tempest,
In the days of the far long ago.

Among the tales that were startling,
Time upon time to me told,
There is one of a most dreadful tempest;
That rages o'er mortal man's soul.

It dawns with sin's tempting pleasure
In the morn, when the soul first awakes;
And thunderous clouds, thickly gather,
While storms on the weary soul breaks.

MORNING SONGS.

The bulwark of life which surrounds it,
'Neath torrents of torture and gall,
'Neath storm-winds of direst temptations,
To oft they are shaken, they fall.

While thicker and dark, grows the tempest,
As the day advances we're told,
The fierce, dreadful winds of temptation,
In torrents they charge on the soul.

The deluge of sin's reenforcements,
With scepter, and missel, and dart,
Joins in with the host of marauders;
In destruction they seek for the heart.

The soldiers grow baffled and weary,
While stifling smoke shadows the air,
The wounded among them are many;
The dying ones groan in despair.

Ere long, when hopes were most vanished,
A cry, but not in despair,
Comes forth from a new reenforcement;
With shouts of defiance, a prayer.

The baffled ones gather about them,
To banish their fear and their dread;
Forthwith to the rampart they follow
The bearer's cross 'bove their heads.

Away flies the evil pursuers,
From the sight of that standard 'tis told,
The thick clouds of gloom and of darkness,
Fall back from their charge on the soul.

MORNING SONGS.

LIFE'S PROCESSION.

They are passing, one by one;
  Morning, noon, at set of sun;
When the dawn awakes the day,
When the noontide shadows play;
Fleeting, like the morning dew,
'Neath the golden sunlight's hue,
In the race of life they run;
They are passing, one by one.

They are passing, one by one;
  Morning, noon, at set of sun;
Through the sunshine and the shade,
Pass the matron and the maid;
Through the vale of death they go,
Through the gloom of bitter woe,
In the race of life they run;
They are passing, one by one.

They are passing, one by one;
  Morning, noon, at set of sun;
Men of wisdom, might, and fame,
Princes, paupers, kings the same;
All, must meet that solemn fate,
All, must pass death's chilling gate
When life's toilsome race is run,
They are passing, one by one.

THE LOCK OF HAIR.

I have in my casket a jewel,
More precious, than rubies or pearl;
'T is only a little blue ribbon,
United, and wove with a curl.

'T is the curl of an Ethiope damsel,
Tinted with deep midnight hue;
A gloss adds fourfold to its beauty,
With a glittering sparkle like dew.

Her tiny black hands plucked this treasure,
From the mass of jet curls on her head,
And they wove in the little blue ribbon;
As a token of fondness, she said.

Her sweet smiles, they haunt me forever,
That curl, and the ribbon of blue,
They ne'er from my casket shall sever;
For I hold them as tokens most true.

FRIENDSHIP'S PARTING.

Ofttimes when friend from friend depart,
A new, sweet fondness touch the heart.
   A feeling so sublime.

'T is but the shaft from cubid's bow,
Which starts love's crimson blood to flow,
   So ends my simple rhyme.

THE NEW YEAR.

Dying, dying, yes he's dying,
Hark! his friends doth crowd around;
See them! lo, they all are crying;
Soon his son shall wear the crown.

Tired and weary are the watchers,
They have watched since early dawn;
Strike the clocks, one hour of midnight,
Soon will dawn the new year's morn.

Slow the clock ticks on the mantle,
Silent gleams the grate's red light,
Bring him water, he is dying;
Soon the soul will take its flight.

Raise him from his couch, he's sinking!
Bind a wet cloth round his head;
Glared and dazed, his eyes cease blinking,
Hark! the old year he is dead.

Bring the shroud, the pall, the bearer!
Death hath rent the parting tear,
Slow and solemn comes the carrier,
Comes the son, the new, new, year.

MORNING SONGS.

On his head, the crown of jewels,
That a thousand kings have worn;
Some too well we know were cruel,
Some were careworn and forlorn.

Mounts he on the monarch's station,
And he smiles with kingly cheer,
As he looks on every nation;
Hark! it is the new, new year.

Drink his health, and spread the table!
Welcome him with mirth and cheer!
Thanks to God, that we are able,
Thus to see another year.

GOLIATH AND DAVID.

Behold the champion of Gath,
   His height, six cubits and a span;
A valorous giant, stern with wrath,
   Defies of Israel, every man.
All glittering gleams his armor bright,
   Aglow doth shine his helmet crest;
Brass greaves encase his legs of might,
   A mammoth gorget shields his breast.

Into his giant hand he holds,
   A spear with staff like weaver's beam;
Oft Israel's host he 've jeered so bold,
   In bantering jest his armor gleams.
For forty days through Elah's vale,
   At dawn of morn, at fall of night,
His challenge with its hideous wail,
   Fell on Saul's host with deathly fright.

Thus spake Goliath, large and tall,
   "Are not ye servants of King Saul,
While I am but a Philistine,
   Why stand ye warriors there serene?
Send down a chosen man from thee,
   And let him come and fight with me!
   And should he overcome my might,
Then we will serve ye Israelites.

But should his strength before me fail,
And o'er him should my strength prevail,
Then thou shalt bow before my host,
And yield thy nation to his lost;"
The men of Israel all gave way,
Beneath Goliath warlike call,
Quoth he, "I do defy this day,
Ye men of Israel, one and all!"

Into the ranks that quaked with fear,
There came a ruddy dauntless lad,
A shepherd's garment he did wear,
A staff, and trusty sling he had;
The tumult broke on David's ear,
Such boastful, scoffing, wrath;
His eyes beheld the ruffian there;
That mighty man of Gath.

"Who is this giant Philistine,
Upon yon slope doth trod,
Why should his shining armor's gleam,
Defy the host of God?
I'm not afraid this man to fight,
My God hath gave me grace;
I care not for his valorous might,
I'll meet him face to face."

"I know thy pride,"brave Eliab said,
   Why camest thou down hither?
Go see that father's flocks be fed!
   Who keepeth them together?"
Again the shepherd spoke the words,
   That fell on one and all,
The captains of the armies heard,
   And brought the news to Saul.

"Go seek that lad,"upspoke King Saul,
   And bring him unto me;
Who says he'll fight Goliath tall;
   I fain his face to see.
Forthwith they brought the shepherd boy,
   Among the warriors frail,
And David said with boastful joy,
   "Of him,let no heart fail!"

Saul said,"thou art a ruddy boy,
   Thou uttereth haughty wrath,
With ease he can thy form destroy,
   This champion of Gath.
"Thy servant watched his father's sheep,
   'Mid fields of Bethlehem,
A lion prowled the forest deep,
   And stole a precious lamb.

I over ran my fleeing foe,
  That robbed my father's fold,
I dealt on him a deadly blow,
  I slew him on the wold;
The Lord who led me forth that day,
  Among those fields of green,
Will give me might, and strength to slay,
  This giant Philistine."

The youth, in coat of mail, Saul armed,
  His armor bright did glow,
The awe struck captains round him swarmed,
  "The Lord be with you, go!"
"Thou hast borne this armor well, my King,
  Thou art a warrior tried,
Give back my shepherd staff and sling,
  I'll cast this coat aside.

For I am but a shepherd lad,
  This sword I dare not cling,
All combats were the Lord's I had,
  I'll meet him with my sling."
As David spake these words profound,
  He dashed the armor to the ground;
Decends the slope, his warlike yell,
  Upon the heathen's host did swell.

He reached the brook and stooping down,
 He chose five bolders, smooth and round;
And one into his sling did lay,
 Went forth, that man of Gath to slay;
Saul's army gave one feeble cheer,
 Goliath, dauntlessly drew near,
His armor bearers 'fore him run,
 His coat of mail reflects the sun.

Its massive weight, a ponderous load,
 He slowly came with stealth he trod,
And seeing David with his rod,
 He cursed him by his heathen Gods;
"Am I a dog, thou Israel slave
That thou shouldst come to me with staves?
Come unto me! thy flesh I'll tear,
To feed the beasts, and fowls of air,"

"Thou cometh mighty man of Gath,"
 The shepherd David said,
"With armor, shield, and greaves of brass,
 And helmet on thy head,
To meet an unarmed shepherd boy,
 To slay him with thy sword,
This day thou giant, I'll destroy;
 This battle is the Lord's.

Thou stands and chide in sullen scorn,
    With vengence, ire, and mirth,
From off thy giant trunk, this morn,
    Thy head, I'll cleave to earth;
And all thy captains and thy host,
    Who scoff ny shepherd rod,
Shall mourn their gallant champion's lost;
    Of Israel, know their God."

These words the mighty champion heard,
    He paid but little heed;
Of Israel, not a man had stirred,
    On David haste with speed;
He plants his feet firm to the ground,
    He halts, he wheels his sling around,
The bolder fled with whizzing sound;
    It sunks deep in Goliath's head;
He groaned, he fell, his bearers fled.

Upon his baffled dying foe,
    The shepherd boy did tread,
And with the champion's sword, one blow,
    Struck off his mighty head;
The host of Israel mad with joy,
    'Rose with tumultuous shout,
They chased, they slaughtered and destroyed,
    They put their foes to rout.

Through vale, o'er hills, and slopes of green,
  Soul's army chased the Philistines;
Until through Ekron gates they went,
Back Israel turned and spoiled their tents;
Now David with his captured prize,
  Turns to Jerusalem;
He bears the head of monstrous size;
  The people gaze with great suprise,
And hail the conqueror's name.

THE JOURNEY OF LIFE.

In our spring,the glorious sunlight,
   Spread his fulgent light abroad;
And her vernal grass,and roses,
   Decorates our pilgrim road.

Roses in their rarest beauty,
   Grasses of an evergreen,
They are placed on special duty
   In this land,by hands unseen.

From the spring,there dawns the summer;
   And fair roses full in bloom,
Soon begins in ceaseless number,
   Dropping petals,one by one.

So our youth doth wax to manhood,
   And the childish face hath fled,
Like the fading roses'petals,
   Fall among the grasses dead.

And as dawns the dreary autumn,
   With its ripened sheaves of grain,
And the sweeping winds are tossing,
   Golden sheaves upon the plain,

Come man's autumn, short the warning,
  Bright hath shone the golden sun,
Day by day, his light grows dimmer;
  Soon life's journey will be done.

Scarcely dawns the fall, till winter,
  Comes with chilling hands so cold,
Garners in the ripened harvest;
  Brings the sheep into the fold.

So man's lot is like the harvest;
  Reaped and stored away on high.
Some like grain that never ripen;
  On the field are left to die.

GO YE UNTO EVERY NATION.

Go ye unto every nation,
    Go before the even tide,
Go with joy and consolation,
    Spread the gospel, far and wide!

Spread it far among the nation;
    Give it to rich and poor;
Leave it at the scoffer's station,
    Hang it on the heathen's door!

Hang the gospel on the highways,
    As a guide post there to lead;
Write with plain and simple letters,
    Though the footsman run, may read!

Go where sick, distressed, where dying;
    Go where wealth and pomp display;
Where the wounded lying, dying;
    Go before the close of day!

Go upon the dark deep ocean;
    Where the sailors tempest tossed;
Tell how Christ in deep devotion,
    Came to save the world, 't was lost!

MORNING SONG.

G•   •ere booms the deadly cannon,
    W• here the musketry doth roar;
W•ere the wounded soldiers' lying,
    Fainting on the fields of gore!

Go within the walls of prison,
    Where the criminals are lead;
Go before the sun hath risen,
    Go before their hopes are fled !

Go until your steps shall falter,
    Go and seek the lost to save;
Till the shroud your mission alter,
    And you 're laid into the grave!

WORK.

Work, ye while the daylight shineth;
　Work, with all thy might and skill;
Work, and ne'er thy task declineth;
　Work, for 'tis our Master's will!

Work, for He hath set thy duty;
　Light the task, how canst thou shirk?
Work, to seek sweet heavenly beauty;
　Ere night cometh, man can't work!

CONTENTS.

CONTENTS.